How to PSILOCYBIN MUSHROOMS

Magic mushroom cultivation

Easy grower's guide book

Leo Holden

Copyright©2016 Leo Holden

All Rights Reserved

Copyright © 2016 by Leo Holden

All rights reserved. No part of this publication may be reproduced, distributed, or transmitted in any form or by any means, including photocopying, recording, or other electronic or mechanical methods, without the prior written permission of the author, except in the case of brief quotations embodied in critical reviews and certain other noncommercial uses permitted by copyright law.

Table of Contents

The magic mushroom is a sentient being	5
Cultivation of mushrooms through the years	10
PSILOCYBIN MUSHROOMS – GENERAL DESCRIPTION	14
Psychotropic chemistry	15
Medical use	19
Types of Psylobes	20
PREPARATION	25
Sterilizing your working area and instruments	28
Substrates and casing	37
SPORE PRINT	40
PREPARING YOUR SPAWN	42
Sterilizing your medium	44
INOCULATION	46
INCUBATION	48
Checking for contaminants	51
FRUITING	52
Casing soil	53
Fruiting chambers	55
Aborts	57
HARVEST	58
Drying and storage	60

Disclaimer

While all attempts have been made to verify the information provided in this book, the author does assume any responsibility for errors, omissions, or contrary interpretations of the subject matter contained within. The information provided in this book is for educational and entertainment purposes only. The reader is responsible for his or her own actions and the author does not accept any responsibilities for any liabilities or damages, real or perceived, resulting from the use of this information.

The trademarks that are used are without any consent, and the publication of the trademark is without permission or backing by the trademark owner. All trademarks and brands within this book are for clarifying purposes only and are the owned by the owners themselves, not affiliated with this document.

The magic mushroom is a sentient being

Hallucinogenic mushrooms are just one of the many delights that nature spread throughout the Earth, for us to indulge into the blissful state of oneness and return with the knowledge of humility and gratitude for being part of this one special manifestation. They bring light unto the sacred interconnectivity of all life cells, dissolving code barriers and implementing a non-discriminative perception of reality. Some call it the revelation of God; others refer to it in more rational, scientific terms, as consciousness expanded to the limit of over-all clarity. For this reason, magic mushrooms have been considered sacred in all parts of the Earth, with cults and rituals devoted to them, revered with overwhelming respect for their mind-blowing capacity - portal to unknown universes, keepers of truth.

Mushrooms like other hallucinogenic plants, used medicinally and ritualistically throughout our history, differ in effect from their chemically refined counterparts, by clearly establishing themselves as an enigmatic presence inside your trip scenario. A mystical guide usually projected as an archetypal figure of the collective unconscious, a spirit of Mother Nature that descended inside you to reveal her beauty, her wisdom and her laws. A universal soul contained in a seemingly plant organism.

But the magic mushroom is a sentient being that has the power to literally blow your brains – atomize your brain structures, in the process of expansion. How can something have such a devastatingly wonderful effect on you? If anything, among hallucinogenic substances, mushrooms is a distinctive force, they grab, drag and throw – they sometimes have the manors of a beast and other times the gracefulness of a fairy. And most often it's the mushroom that has a message for you; it almost calls you every time. You obey its will; therefore you must befriend it, for its ways to be smooth and clear.

When growing magic mushrooms you become aware of this aspect, of the intelligent life form evolving under your eyes. They fruit with such a rapid pace, that you can watch them appearing and maturing live – it's an incredible spectacle, you only turn your head for a second and it's a whole new setup with different characters, new mushrooms have just popped up at the party, while veterans are already growing their hats. Life in all is beauty.

And you have to talk to your mushrooms, transfer energy and information. Send them love and they will respond tenfold. Take care of them and they will grow in their entire splendor, neglect them and they might turn to the dark side.

(Not saying that the dark side isn't an essentially necessary level, but pointing out that distress manifests as spectacularly in the growth of the mushrooms as well as inside your mind)

The present guide will introduce you to the life cycles of a psychotropic fungus, exploring the transformations that take place from the moment of germination till fruiting mushrooms. It's a complex journey that needs to be understood before anything. The cultivation itself is an art and a ritual that one must address with a clear mind and an open soul.

You will be familiarized with most of the techniques of growing magic mushrooms that have been devised till now, but I will focus on the simplest method, one that will provide the novice a mean to start learning by experiencing.

Mushrooms have a magical tendency to thrive when you least expect them and need nothing more than nature itself provides for them. For me they worked wonders in the hardest conditions. That is why I recommend growing them with hope in your heart and trusting that they will evolve miraculously.

Although I mentioned specific nutrients and chemical compounds that would help in the over-all process, I strongly point that if you have good substrate and soil, if you take enough care in sterilization and are aware of what your mushrooms need, it's more than enough for your culture to succeed.

Cultivation of mushrooms through the years

The growing of mushrooms has not been such a wide spread phenomenon, neither worldwide, nor during the history of men kind. This may be partly because they are so prolific natural organisms that don't miss the chance to fruit season after season, enduring rough geographical and weather conditions; and partly because of their highly mutable nature.

Being organisms that reproduce by spreading spores, they modify their structure in inter-dependence with the other species of mushrooms co-habiting the same area. For example, in some years the toxicity in a forest can reach great levels, as registered in its "poisonous" specimens that develop to a remarkable degree of potency. In those years, even the most experienced edible mushrooms gatherers are in the risk of getting intoxicated – as a result of the spore and thus gene exchange in the air as well as higher concentration of certain substances in the soil, the edible mushrooms became toxic in their turn.

Being microorganism, fungus can be easily influenced by other microorganisms like bacteria or mold and ultimately annihilated in the quest for food and survival.

The soil, the substrate that supports the growth, has to be nutritious and compatible.

And most importantly the medium, in which they grow, from inoculation to maturity, has to be free of dangerous contaminants.

In wilderness the mushrooms thrive wherever they find perfect conditions.

But as you can see, when attempting to cultivate mushrooms, there are a lot of coordinates to take into consideration.

If it's outside, it should be a place that mostly resembles its natural habitat (in terms of clime, temperature, humidity, altitude, and host as in the surrounding with its specific flora). If inside, than it should be completely sterile (operation room type of aseptic)

Even the edible mushrooms were only to be found wild, until recent years when people developed methods to improvise efficient farming. In the past, there were only a few cultures around the globe that have pursued such practice, some in Europe, some in the Americas and China, in caves or outdoor on logs, depending of the mushroom type.

The growing process used back then resembles a lot with the techniques used today, as core strategy and understanding. But the means to sterilize the cultivation room and acclimatize it to simulate natural conditions have improved remarkably.

One of the first books to introduce the cultivation of magic mushrooms to the public was *Psilocybin: Magic Mushroom Grower's Guide*, written by O.T. Oss and O.N. Oeric, which are pseudonyms for the well-known psychonauts, the McKenna brothers. This is in a way the manual that almost all growers read at one point, because, even if it's old already and some of the recommended techniques have been improved, it explains in details every aspect and it still constitutes the basic starting point for any method of cultivation practiced today.

The method discussed in this guide is also very similar to the one used over 40 years ago by the psychedelic explorers.

One other interesting technique was introduced in the '90's in the book called The Psilocybe Fanaticus Technique that taught about growing Psilocybe Cubensis on brown rice and vermiculite. This kind of airy substrate permits the fungus to expand rapidly and uniformly, it also needs less care in sterilizing, thus it can be a very good method for a novice to start observing and learning live through all the stages of the process. But it is not a recommendable substrate to use for more than one batch, as it is also very low in nutrients, therefor the mushrooms will lack in terms of potency.

PSILOCYBIN MUSHROOMS – GENERAL DESCRIPTION

What we call magic mushroom is actually the fruit of a fungus, a multicellular microorganism, with specific features and habits that place it apart from plants and animals, in its own kingdom.

Domain Eukarya, kingdom Fungi, phylum Basidiomycota, class Hymenomycotina, order Agaricales, family Strophariaceae. Most of the psychedelic mushrooms are a part of the genus Psilocybe and Panaeolus with some in the Gymnopilus, Inocybe, and Conocybe.

From more thirty thousand specie of fungi that fruit into mushroom, just about one hundred contain psychotropic substances and still most of them, in quantities so small that makes them inefficient to our psyche.

Psychedelic mushrooms can be found virtually all over the Earth, in a variety of appearances, potencies and variations in the quality of the trip as well as several specie occurring with small differences on different continents.

Psychotropic chemistry

The psycho-active compounds that deliver us the opportunity to enter and explore other realms of life, by switching us into awareness, are psilocybin and psilocin. Their configuration constitutes the basic indole structure blueprint that is also integrated by most psychedelics provided by nature – same as in some amides of lysergic acid (LSD – in its synthetically refined form), ibogaine, and harmine.

The reason that they have such an amazing effect on us is because our chemistries overlap – the structure of the mushroom's active agents is mirrored by the brain's own regulating compounds, as the indole amine neuro-hormones – melatonin and serotonin – that coordinate the circadian rhythms, the mood equilibrium, sleep and appetite patterns.

Pic 1. Melatonin

Pic.2 Serotonin

Psilocybin and psilocin trigger specific serotonergic receptors inside our body in order to distort the neural network, infusing it with fresh energy. Targeted are the 5-HT receptors in the human body (serotonin is a 5-HT neurotransmitter – 5-hydroxytriptamine). And mostly affected is the 5-HT2 receptors found in the brain, cardiovascular system, immune system, gastrointestinal system. Due to this brain interactivity, routine processes are transformed, like the allowing for much more informational input through sensory gates, the mechanism of translating and integrating information which is also boosted, the learning mechanism is furthered and the visual sensitivity is heightened.

Pic 3 Psilocin

Medical use

Psilocybin has been used ritualistically to spiritually overcome physical and psychological impediments, that block or diminish the strength of the connection between your own cells and the universal source.

Modern medicine has integrated it as transformative agent, able to relieve states of acute depression – researches done in this area specify its efficiency as higher than conventional medication prescribed for this type of condition.

One other way that this magical psychotropic compound is incorporated by the medical practice, is as aid given to patients in the final states of a terminal disease, to ease their passing process and free them from the fear of death.

From scientific analysis emerges one other revolutionary theory – not only that psilocybin doesn't damage the brain cells, but instead, it promotes their growth and regeneration.

Thus, ingesting magic mushrooms is more than anything, a therapeutic practice.

Types of Psylobes

Among them, there is one specie that has been most cultivated, **Psilocybe Cubensis**. This is the one mushroom specie that mesmerized the travelers that attended a ritual in Mexico and returned to the West with this knowledge, a historical moment that constituted the rediscovery of its whole family.

Psilocybe Cubensis is to be found worldwide, as one of the most frequently encountered psychotropic specie. It is also one strong adaptable mushroom that can resist harsh conditions. But it's highly appreciated for it is so easy to grow on a wide variety of substrates – different grains, corn, grasses; wood, paper or even cardboard has been tried. Though any substrate should be nourished with a high amount of nitrogen and carbon, as well as proteins.

Psilocybe Cubensis thrives in tropical climates and fruits as much as the weather permits and as long as there are nutrients in its soil. Thus is not so easy to cultivate outdoors, unless in an environment that resembles its native lands, where this specific mushroom is so wide spread that its cultivation becomes superfluous.

It is not very potent, among its siblings, it contains up to 1.2% psilocybin, psilocin, baeocystin.

For outdoor cultivation, some of its relatives are more appropriate, as these ones grow on wood, logs or chips, as well as bark mulch. These are the so-called **caramel-capped Psylobes**: Psilocybe cyanescens, Psilocybe azurescens (both native in North America), Psilocybe serbica and Psilocybe bohemica (from Eastern Europe), Psilocybe sub aeruginosa and Psilocybe tasmania (in Australia and New Zeeland).

These types of Psilocybe are also some of the most potent psychedelic mushrooms out there with concentrations of up to 2.5 % of psilocybin, though they appear considerably smaller and less abundant in fruits than cubensis.

All of them are very similar, when addressing their cultivation, as they require same environmental conditions and go through more or less identical stages.

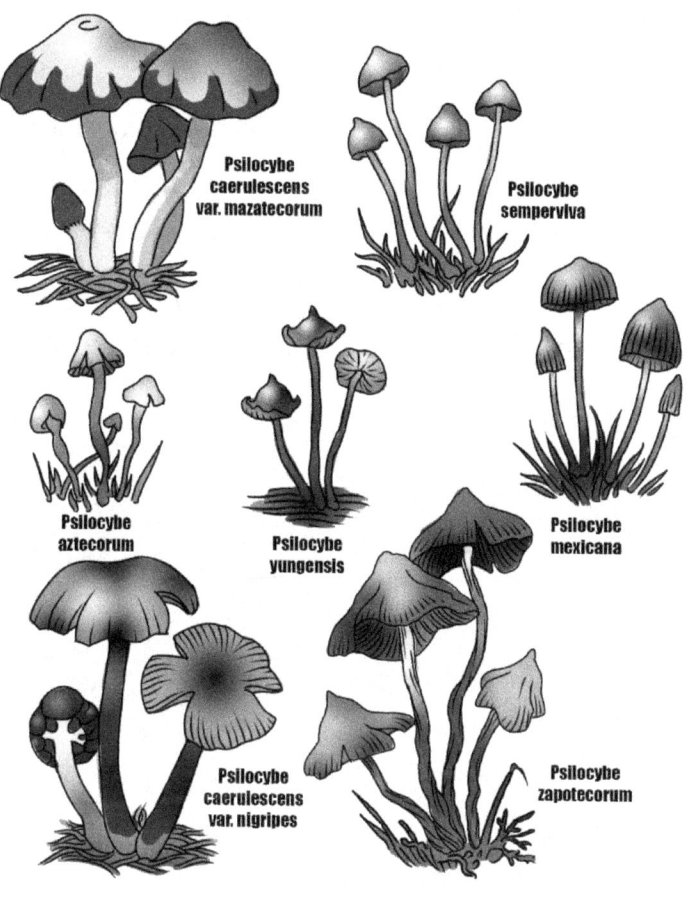

Almost all psycho-active mushrooms are bruised when ripped apart as well as when just pressed on their stipe or cap and turn blue in that area. This is a sign of their psilocybin concentration, as this substance colors the flesh of the fruited fungus as it oxidases.

! This is by no means to be read backwards – not every mushroom that turns blue when pressed is psychotropic specie. A lot of other specie oxidase in different colors (from the more frequent blue and green, to orange and red). In fact, according to popular belief, this is a proof of its toxicity – which is also valid for extremely poisonous, lethal mushrooms that have no psychedelic affect whatsoever!

PREPARATION

With the risk of sounding annoying, I must repeat that the most important aspect in mushroom cultivation is keeping your environment free of contaminants. This is as well the main set-back when you want to engage in such an action because you have to be tremendously careful, wear gloves and sterilize everything constantly – yourself, the instruments, the working place, the mushrooms space. Before each step you take, sanitizing is a must. You'll repeat this routine more than one time a day in some stages and countless more throughout the whole process, that it will enter your system like a mantra. Besides that, mushroom cultivation needs a lot of time, energy and most of all attention.

Thus, growing the magic mushrooms is a ritual in itself – in the course of it you'll get accustomed to the chloride and sanitary alcohol smell, it will also teach you discipline, it will sometimes exhaust you, but nevertheless, it will enrich you and gratify you, during the process and of course at the end when you'll be able to enjoy the magical treats.

Almost all the cases when something went wrong, was when contaminants have succeeded to infiltrate the growing space. And it's a disastrous picture with the substrate turning all slimy, in an impressive palette of wrong colors, from brown to black, green and even orange, covered in mold and smelling like the devil died inside there. It can be truly traumatizing after such an effort and mostly first time ends up like this invariably. That is why most give up after one try, but be prepared to persevere.

My first batch was contaminated even before I was supposed to move the mycelium in the fruiting cell. It was swampy brown, stinking and leaking so I threw it all away. Or at least I thought so, but later on I discovered that I forgot two jars in a corner, in an area that was exposed to day light. When I found them, one jar was in an even more advanced stage of degradation, but in the other one, the mycelium has fruited me some beautiful but a bit tormented mushrooms. They have grown inside the jar, in such a small space that they evolved all cramped up, twisted and squeezed against themselves as well as against the walls of the jar.

It was an incredible surprise and I was even more amazed by the high potency of those little beasts and the good smooth flow of the trip, more like what you would expect from a healthy well taken care of batch. But seemingly my abandoned mushrooms were there to encourage me to go on trying and do my best, as they have done for me this time.

Sterilizing your working area and instruments

Most of the actions will be undertaken inside a glove box. Nevertheless you will also need a working room that should be properly disinfected and a working table with a surface that will allow you to wipe it with alcohol before every use. Best choice is the bathroom if you have enough space, because it's the most easy to clean area from the whole house. Remember we are talking about myriads of microscopic particles that are usually floating around in any environment, from dust to pollen grains, and most damaging, mold spores. That is why you should definitely avoid the kitchen area, unless you're prepared to sterilize its every inch, every time you use it; and the basement or garage, that are usually infused with mold.

Empty the room, clean it along with all objects that will get back in, sterilizing afterwards with a chloride solution. You may even need to repaint a bit, cramps in the walls blow small dust particles into the air. Get rid of all objects that are inhabited by contaminants, particularly the plants, pet's beds and litters. Carpets are also a perfect environment for bacteria to thrive.

Could be useful to acquire HEPA air filtration equipment that can eliminate solid matter from the air, with a performance of 99,97%.

Before work, close all windows and block even the smallest drafts of air, puff the chloride solution spray a few times in the air and leave it for 10 minutes before going in.

Needless to say, you also have to be sterile, freshly showered, in fresh clothes. Wear short sleeves and shirts that are not too loose, so as not to accidently gets a piece of textile touching your instruments or your batch. Keep your hair tied on your head. Wear surgical gloves and wipe them, as well as your lower arms, with isopropyl alcohol before getting to work.

The instruments that you will use have to be sterilized – the preferred method is using a pressure cooker (one essential item that you'll make use of repeatedly). At 121° C (255° F) and 15 psi you can be sure no living organism survives.

Although with everything that needs your assistance, this may come as simply too much – getting yourself in the right state of mind is a crucial aspect. Essentially because your attention has to be focused and each action has to be precise and done in the quickest manner – at all stages, mycelium has to be exposed to the room environment for the shortest period of time so every action has to follow up rapidly one after the other.

On another hand, a luminous and awakened state of perception grants you the necessary concentration and infuses the miraculous beings you're growing with similar energy.

What you need

It's not like you need an entire chemistry lab to grow psychotropic mushrooms, but there are a few essential items that you can't do without.

Pressure cooker – has to be large enough to contain a few jars, the bigger the better. When using it, you should let it build up heat slowly and always bring it to a full head of steam, closing the stop-cock only afterwards, this way it will warm evenly on its entire surface. A constant pressure is required for sterilizing. Before opening it, it must cool down on its own – otherwise a sudden change of pressure can make it implode and you may wake up with the cap violently hitting your face, to say the least.

Bottles for keeping the liquid media in the sterilization process – pre-sterilized plastic bottles or glass ones that can be autoclaved.

Jars – 500g jars will do. The important parts are the lid and the filter disc that should be made out of materials able to resist through the process of sterilization.

The lids should be modified in order to permit the exchange of air. To do so, drill 4 small holes.

The filter disc is a sheath used for the purpose of filtrating impurities that come through the pierced lid. It is usually made out of heat resistant synthetic fiber. You can also improvise it yourself, one adequate material is Tyvek, and for sure you can find others.

If you don't manage to find or devise filter discs, there is one way to do without. It's more hazardous, but it worked for me. Instead of drilling just 4 holes, pierce it in more places all over its surface, with a very thin needle like instrument. Than place over its cap, a piece of aluminum foil. It's far less secure than the filter disc, but with a bit of luck it would do its job.

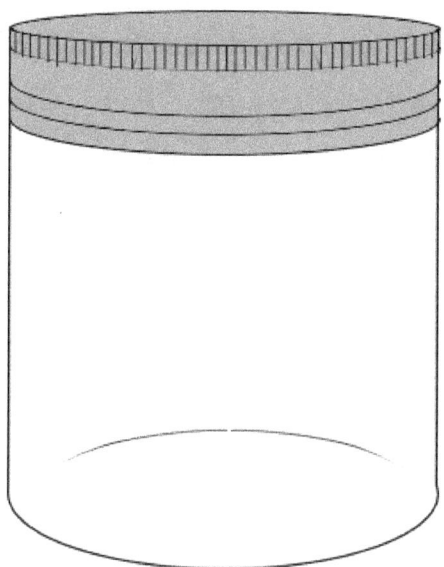

Fruiting chamber – box, bag, jar or other type of container that will keep your spawn. The item that growers usually prefer for this, is a filter patch bag, made from plastic that can be sterilized in the pressure cooker and heat sealed, having a small filter for air exchange, embedded on one side.

You can also use chloride solution to sterilize your box. It is less protective than, but with a meticulous cleaning of every inch and every corner, you could decontaminate it.

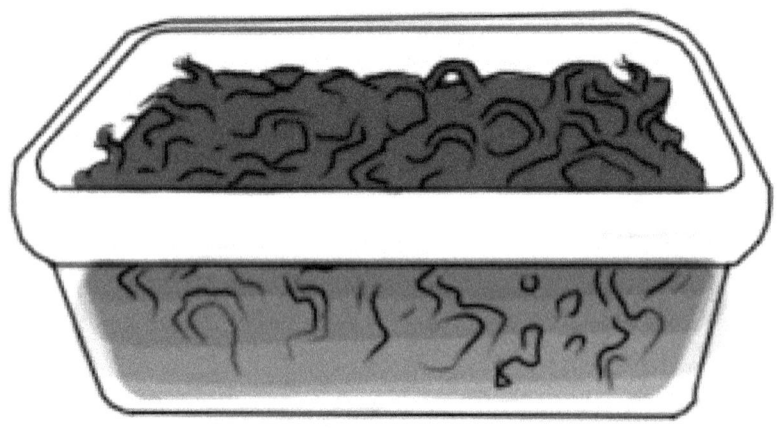

Alcohol lamp, monitors on butane gas or a simple lighter – for sterilizing metal instruments as you work.

Scalpel – for cutting tissue culture or agar. An aluminum knife can work well also.

Inoculation loop – a wire that has a loop at one end, you can do it yourself from thin wire. Or you can also use the scalpel or the knife for inoculation, though these imply a bit roughly and imprecise handling.

Syringes – used for spore inoculation

Surgical gloves

Chloride solution

Isopropyl alcohol

Although this will not be used in the method explained in this guide, as we work with spores and it is harmful for them, it is worth mentioning:

Hydrogen Peroxide (3%) *– this is a substance that helps the fungus repent contaminators and naturally protect itself. It works as an antiseptic without interfering with the growth.*

Substrates and casing

Whole grains are the most common choice of substrate for producing spawn, used afterwards to inoculate bulk mycelium. This is a medium that innately contains the nutrients and minerals that the fungus needs to form mycelium, moreover they can be infused and keep enough water to sustain the necessary humidity. One of its characteristics that make it such an efficient substrate is its aerated structure that permits it to be easily colonized.

Most used grains are rye, wheat, corn and rice (brown or wild rice, that won't turn sticky when cooked). Rye is particularly a preferred option because it is more nutritious and it appears to be able to absorb a larger amount of water without getting its protective shell too moistened. From experience, mycelium itself enjoys it as it colonizes it very rapidly (when properly prepared), in a uniformed texture and if you shake it regularly you can get it broken evenly.

__Calcium sulfate (gypsum)__ is one miraculous ingredient that if added to the substrate will take care of the surplus of water by absorbing it, which will permit an overall even level of humidity. It also makes it easier to separate the mycelium-grains, when trying to break it. And most of all it deters contaminants.

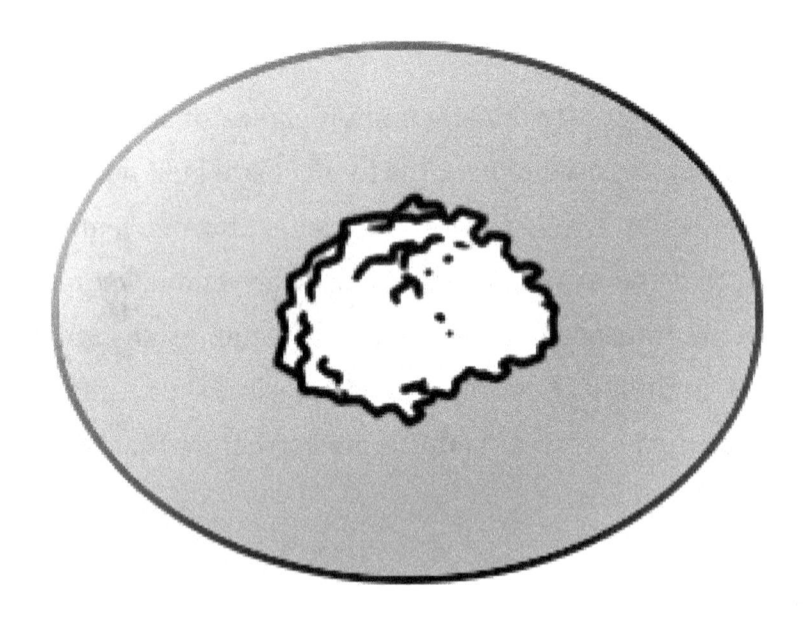

Casing soil is usually gardening soil or forest soil, as in the surface layer, just underneath the leaves cover.

There are two components used to help the casing soil retain a higher amount of water without sinking it, but instead releasing it bit by bit. One of them is **vermiculite** which is also a constituent part of the casing soil – it is important because its structure makes the soil more aerated. And **water crystals** which are able to contain a huge amount of water.

If you feed your substrate and your casing soil calcium, by adding **Calcium carbonate (chalk)** it will turn it into a more basic medium. This will benefit your fungus, as for contaminants, they like it more acidic so they will exit the scene.

SPORE PRINT

Of course the easiest way is to buy the spores. But in some way it's also the most difficult, so it's best to learn how to take them yourself from a fresh mushroom.

The spores are formed underneath the barium, on the mushroom's gills. To take spores you need a healthy specimen with the cap wide open. You should cut its stem by approximating that when placing the cap with its gills underneath, it should have a buffer of 1-2 mm till the ground surface. Cut it straight so it won't be hanging on one side more than another.

Spores are best imprinted on aluminum or glass, as these are surfaces that are not porous thus can be easily sterilized and particles can be easily collected with an inoculation loop.

Clean the surface with a piece of cotton soaked in alcohol and let it dry, then places the cap of the mushroom. Cover it with some bigger container, this should keep the inside environment humid enough.

When growing and spreading naturally, the wild mushroom follows more or less the same steps - its cap maintains a high humidity underneath it therefore its gills are covered in a thin layer of moist; very small drops begin to form around the spores and when they are heavy enough, they simply fall and along with them the spores too. The spores are afterwards carried away by the wind.

Same thing when imprinting them, only hopefully this time there will be no wind to blow them away.

After a few hours the spore print should be completed, but to be safe, better leave it overnight.

When taking them to mix in the liquid inoculation solution, just use the loop (pre-sterilized in alcohol and fire) and it only needs one touch to grab huge amount of spores that you will dilute with water. For this, place the spores in 10 ml of sterilized water, close the container and shake well, then dilute it by adding more sterilized water up to 100 ml.

PREPARING YOUR SPAWN

Before we go into the practical methodology let's go over the natural processes that take place at the starting of a colony, this will give you a better understanding of the stages that the fungus goes through and thus of aspects to take care of when artificially inducing its development.

Once inoculated the mycelium will start growing, expanding radially from each inoculation point, as a result of the germination of the spores into monokaryotic mycelium (one nucleus per cell). It grows until it meets another monokaryotic mycelium, that is a compatible mating type and the perfect match is found, a phenomenon called somatogamy takes place. In the course of this event, all of the cells (except the nuclei) of both myceliums fusion, transforming into a dikaryotic mycelium (two nuclei per cell). At the moment of an established colony, mycelium enters in a vegetative stage that can last virtually endlessly, if conditions are maintained.

Here, we will discuss growing spawn on grains, as this unprocessed substrate already contains everything that is needed for the fungus to catch life and expand its mycelium. It doesn't need any other substances as food, nor for protection. What is recommended to add extra (like gypsum or chalk) is only to potentiate the growth and sturdiness of the fungus and to make your job easier. In truth, all there's needed it's imprinted genetically in the spores, so we'll move on with the option that is more similar to what fungi would choose in their natural environment – in this case, grains.

Usually mushroom growers produce their spawn on an agar media mostly because it simplifies the whole process. Its gelatinous texture makes the mycelium spread fast and this type of structure makes it easier to control contamination. On the other hand agar lacks nutritious compounds, its sugar based extract from algae, so you must pump it yourself with everything your fungus needs.

! Any medium you use for spawn, either is agar or grains, it should only be for a limited period. After a number of generations, the gene begins to grow old and this can be observed in the mushroom fruits that become weaker and fewer. This phenomenon is called senescence and it can't quite be explained. But it's best to change the spawn medium from time to time in order to revive your cultures!

Sterilizing your medium

Cereals tend either to be populated by a large number of different types of bacteria, harmless for humans but devastating for fungus – if organically cultivated; either to be infused with large amounts of chemicals (mostly coming from pesticides) – in the case of the no-restrictions monocultures. You can get rid of the undesired bacteria but the chemicals are there to stay and they kill the fungus, so it's almost a must to get it from an organic farmer.

Sterilization happens in the pressure cooker, but before that you have to prepare your grains for the process. This is an important step because it helps to eliminate contaminators.

The grains need to be soaked in a little water over night, and then the whole quantity is transferred into a cooking pot. Add water, twice the volume occupied by grains and put it to a full boil for 10 minutes. Then let it rest for at least 8 hours. To check if it's ready hydrated, take a grain between your fingers and press it to feel if the inside texture is uniformly soft. If it's all good to go, the grains should be thoroughly drained.

! One thing you must pay attention to is the surface of the grains and if it's gluey then you have to carefully rinse it in cold water!

Add the gypsum and the chalk to the party. You have to mix them very well without squashing the grains so put it all in a pot that you can seal with its cap and shake it softly on all sides.

Then transfer it to the containers that will go in the pressure cooker. After cooking at 15 psi for 90 minutes, sterilization has happened. Take them off the oven but leave them chill inside the pressure cooker till you're ready to inoculate them.

Quantities for 250 ml jars:

Grain – 250 ml

Calcium sulfate (gypsum) – 1 g (1/4 tbsp.)

Calcium carbonate (chalk) – 1 g (1/4 tbsp.)

INOCULATION

You can inoculate your grain substrate in various ways, most easily is to transfer a very small quantity of mycelium from an already colonized source, which may be grains as well as agar. This is why when growing constantly you'll find it suitable to maintain a source.

But as I suppose that you start with almost nothing, I'll present the method of **spore syringe inoculation** and it goes like this:

You will use a 10 ml syringe and inject 2-3 ml of spore solution per inoculation point; therefore the content of one syringe will be enough to inoculate 1 maximum 2 jars.

The jars are taken out of the pressure cooker and placed inside the glove box. (Remember that whenever you use the box you have to disinfect it first, so give the chloride spray a few puffs). Loosen the lids on the jars just a little bit to allow air exchange.

Wipe the needle with a piece of cotton or textile that's been soaked in alcohol and then put it in a fire flame till it turns red. Use it after it cools to its original color.

Your lids already have tiny holes (preferably four) – stick the needle through the holes, measuring to inject the same quantity in each.

INCUBATION

As a measure of securing the successful growth of mycelium and control the timing and strict conditions, growers use incubators. Which in fact are not at all hard to make, you only need a few things from any general supply store and if you're a handy man by nature, be a generous soul and help others do it also.

But there is of course the possibility of living the nature to take its own course, even though it means slowing down the process and making it last a bit longer. For me it worked perfectly to leave them in a corner of the living room. If you keep them at 65-80? ° F °C and protected from air currents, the fungus will grow beautifully. This is granted by the fact that in the course of growing, mycelium generates itself heat, making the temperature inside the jar a few degrees higher than outside. Of course the process will last much longer, up 24 days.

A few days or at most a week after inoculation you can begin to see the first expanding cells of the white strains of mycelium.

When you inoculate your substrate from each of the points of injection, the fungus will start growing monokaryotic mycelium. And as we've seen the mating sequence is essential for the survival of the mycelium, so it's best to be left undisturbed until we're sure somatogamy has taken place. Theoretically this is evident when the myceliums from two inoculation points have merged. But practically, you don't need to wait that long because each point was infused with such a large amount of spores that most probably they have found their mates among their own. So when the mycelium strings have turned more ropey and it seems overall formed and only then, you can give it its first shake. (Be sure to close the lid first)

That's why it's more simple when inoculating with a piece of spawn than with spores, as it's already dikaryotic mycelium that your infiltrating and it takes over the substrate in a much shorter time.

Shaking the jars – to further the growth, speed up the colonization. This way you break the bigger chunks and redistribute them in order for it to spread evenly in the whole jar.

Although some say that you should start shaking when your initial mycelium dots have reached strains of about 1 cm, but from my experience this action rather slows down the growth at this early stage. I've observed that it's best to wait till about one third of the entire substrate is colonized. Otherwise you break down structures that are only beginning to form and send the fungus a step backwards.

In this process of colonization, the mycelium expands, consuming the grains and binding them tightly together. So it sometimes becomes really difficult to break apart. But generally, if the substrate is prepared properly, it will invariably break. If you need to band the jar to displace the content do it first slightly by slapping it with your hand and if you still require something stronger to bang it on – it should preferably be a wood object and the jar should be covered in a towel.

Although it's much better to be perseverant, as there's the risk that your jar might crack.

The jars are to be shaken once every 5 days.

Checking for contaminants

Once every few days you should inspect each jar thoroughly to search if it hasn't been contaminated. It's necessary to detect in time, and separate the infected jar from the clean ones, as mold particles spread rapidly through the air, through filter discs and into the other substrates.

So look around the surface of the jar and see if there is any visible sign of mold, like spots of any type of color (mycelium of Psylobe mushrooms is white so any other nuance is excluded). And also pay attention to wet areas, either grains covered in a water bubble or water drops on the surface of the jar – this is frequently the first sign of contamination.

A good way to check if everything's alright, it to sniff the jar and sense it any dubious smell, if it's starting to rot, it will smell as though fermented.

It is quite crucial to take extra prudence when it comes to contamination. Molds are more sturdy and viral than fungus; they can take over an entire colony in a few days, exactly how long it takes you between two check-ups. So check twice better than having a nasty surprise.

FRUITING

Mycelium is induced into fruiting mainly when exposed to light. Though it needs much more water to develop its fruiting body, light is the trigger.

You can either use the same jars or transfer the spawn to a box or some other bigger container. If you want to use the same jars, be sure to fill them with substrate leaving one third empty - this volume will be needed to add the casing soil.

The box is a more efficient option because the mycelium layer can be much thinner so as to cover a larger surface for a larger number of mushrooms. Before you transfer the mycelium is sure to sterilize the box, by whipping it with chloride solution. When placing the mycelium, break it into small chunks and spread them evenly, then leave it to reestablish itself by growing and binding the pieces into one mass.

Only then you can cover it with casing soil.

Casing soil

Using it is not a must, you can do without. But it is extremely beneficial to you fungus culture, because it promotes a uniform fruiting on an even texture, it maintains humidity and constitutes a barrier for contaminants. One other special add that comes with the casing soil is an extra load of nutrients that your mushrooms will be grateful for.

For me, everything worked out perfectly even when employing the most primal preparations - just emptying the spawn jar inside the box and leaving it as it is, not breaking it into smaller pieces, although the mycelium had grown in such a strong bond that it came out as one complete chunk. It fruited on its entire surface beautifully. All I had to do after harvest is break it in two parts to refresh it, then after the second fruiting; brake it again and so on.

Mushrooms need humidity, but not a swampy environment so you must moisturize your soil, but are careful not to sink it in water. Spread it on a straight surface and level it. Spray it with water using a small hose, checking by pressing it between your fingers and if it keeps its form, then it's ready. The key is to maintain humidity but under no circumstance to allow water leaking into the mycelium.

After establishing the perfect level of humidity, the casing soil must be sterilized in the pressure cooker.

Fruiting chambers

Whether it's done in jars or in a box, the fruiting stage needs a set of special conditions, more specifically a perfect equilibrium has to be reached between temperature, humidity and ventilation. A warm environment and light are necessary to induce and promote fruiting. The mycelium also consumes larger quantities of water, as it perspires and integrates it in its growing fruiting body. Ventilation is crucial for the health and strength of the mushrooms. The state of balance of each of these three coordinates depends on the other two.

So after transferring the mycelium to the fruiting box, humidity will be maintained by spraying the interior with water once a day. If you use casing soil, you can sprinkle to get it moist. If not, then it's a bit harder because you only spray the walls, paying attention not drop water on mycelium (if a few drops do fall, than tampon the area softly with a napkin). You must constantly look at the walls and if there are no more water drops on the interior, it means that the humidity level has dropped below your needed standard.

To ensure a good air exchange, you can open the box once every 2 days, take the cap off and swing it a few times above it to ventilate the inside air.

In about 2-3 weeks, the mycelium will grow into the casing layer but stop underneath the surface. One reason of constantly spraying the soil is specifically to maintain it humid enough so as to block the expansion of mycelium above. If it does break through it will form a crust that will make fruiting a difficult process.

The expansion of mycelium at the exterior is actually a sign of poor ventilation

You will be able to see the network of mycelium turning more and more ropey and covering the entire surface from one side to another. At the points where strands intersect, white dots will be visible, marking the appearance of the fruiting bodies.

From that moment, growth will happen extremely rapid, the mushrooms reaching maturity within 5-10 days.

It's a live show that cannot be described in words. You feel like watching them for the entire period.

Aborts

Every batch has a considerable amount of aborts, mushrooms that have not evolved properly but remained small, short, some so minuscule that are really hard to spot. It's likely a natural phenomenon of selection.

Aborts can be much stronger than a mature healthy mushroom as they apparently concentrate more potency.

When harvesting it's very important to be sure that you collect all the aborts in a generation, because they constitute an invitation and a host for contaminants. You may need to scratch the mycelium with a scalpel to efficiently remove some of them.

Contamination is still a threat in this stage as well as all others, maybe more now because more air exchange is needed. And particular care is mandatory because molds can take over you culture very fast.

So pay attention to any blue green dots and when you spot one take it out with the pre-sterilized scalpel. Usually if you see areas with water accumulation is a sign that the mycelium has been infected in that place.

HARVEST

A mycelium culture is not exhausted after only one fruiting, but can be used multiple times. After a while you will start noticing that it grew out of nutrients and discard. But to ensure its longevity you have to harvest in time otherwise you risk the mycelium becoming toxic and also losing your entire yield.

The time is right when the first mushroom has opened its cap, as it is a collective trigger for the entire generation, no matter what individual stage of growth they're in. When one did it, all will follow up in no time.

It may sometimes happen that the fungus decides to send its fruiting body downwards to the bottom of the box, missing the chance to reach above the surface into the air. It's a bit of a restrictive if not suffocating way to grow and it messes up your whole structure. To avoid this event, wrap the mycelium part of the box in aluminum foil, this will keep the light from inducing fruiting all over that area.

Anyway, once you've harvested them and before indulging in the unique pleasure of eating the fresh sample of your personal mushroom, you can take spores from the second best specimen (the first is for your psychedelic trip) and prepare the others for drying and ultimately storage.

Drying and storage

To dry your harvest you can either place it in a special drying chamber or in a room with good ventilation and away from direct sunlight. When the mushrooms crack at pressing, they're dried.

It's best to store them in plastic bags that are vacuumed and sealed, especially if it's for longer periods of time. But you can also keep them in paper bags if they're destined for next full moon ritual.

Another way to store is to place mushrooms into honey substance. Honey will prevent your mushrooms from oxygen. Oxygen is really harmful for psilocybin and psilocin. Moreover honey is the only one product that never spoils. So you can save your psilocybes forever.

The entire process from the first moment of spore imprinting till when you bite the head of the most beautiful of your mushrooms, takes about 60 days.

The art of growing magic mushrooms is one that is learned through practice. It's also precious knowledge that demands to be shared and experienced collectively, much in the way that the psilocybin trip expands our consciousness by connecting us.

! Always share your fruits, of your mind as well as your fungus!

CPSIA information can be obtained
at www.ICGtesting.com
Printed in the USA
LVHW051305141220
674120LV00037B/563

9 781541 228023